Journeys
to a
Higher Destination

Stories of People Finding Their True Purpose

SHELTON H. SMITH JR.

ISBN 978-1-64492-843-1 (paperback)
ISBN 978-1-64492-844-8 (digital)

Christian Faith Publishing, Inc.
832 Park Avenue
Meadville, PA 16335
www.christianfaithpublishing.com

Printed in the United States of America

To my Lord and Savior, Jesus Christ. Without Him, I am nothing.

To my wife, Marie, who has not only walked beside me in life, but has often had to *carry* me.

To my son, my namesake, of whom I am so proud, and to my daughter, Ashley, whose knowledge, efforts, and guidance have helped bring my dream of authorship to fruition... *I love you all!*

Rev. Shelton H. Smith Jr.
Chesapeake, VA
December 2015

Contents

Preface

In the heart of every human being, there is a hunger—a hunger for knowledge, increase, and advancement. This hunger and passion to move forward and gain more in life drives us to seek the unknown.

In our quest to be better, we often surround ourselves with the pleasures in life that we believe will bring joy and satisfaction—things like wealth, large homes, expensive cars, status in the community, and power. These things do bring a sense of satisfaction to our lives, but unfortunately, it's only temporary. Because of this, we continue to reach for more...only to find that the end result is the same.

On the journey of life, I've found that what my head tells me is quite often not true, but when I listen to my heart—that inner voice of the Holy Spirit—I'm never wrong. To succeed in life, we must learn to gravitate to the Spirit and not to our own thoughts and desires.

This book is about the journeys of several different people to find the real truth they so desperately need. I can identify with each of these stories in one way or another. I too, have had obstacles, medical and personal issues, disappointments, and all the highs and lows that life brings, but one day, the Savior met me where I was and took me by the hand, pulled me from the sand I was sinking in, and gave me a new spirit.

To God be the glory!

Rev. Shelton H. Smith Jr.
Chesapeake, Virginia
December 2015

Tommy's Wake-up Call

For Tommy, life is sweeter every morning when he wakes up. The days seem brighter, the air smells fresher, and even his food seems to taste better! He thanks God for every minute that He gives. Each day, he tries to take note of something he hasn't seen before, do something he's never done before, or experience something he never experienced before.

Now, just in case you think he's a little strange or "off his rocker," he's not. You see, he's been given a *second chance* at life. He hasn't always felt this good or this positive. Admittedly, this is all new for Tommy. He used to be angry and resentful. Then the Lord woke him up.

Tommy was a manager of a restaurant in his town and had been in food service for over seventeen years. He enjoyed his career even when he first started by cleaning tables and mopping floors. Over the years, he worked his way up to manager of the restaurant and was very proud of his accomplishments. He planned to stay in the food service business and hoped to own his own restaurant one day.

He truly loved his career. He enjoyed every aspect of the restaurant business all the way down to dealing with difficult customers... most of the time. Tommy also enjoyed the nightlife. He regularly hung out with friends after work, hopping from one bar to the next, meeting tons of different women, and partying until the sun came up. Tommy embraced this hectic life and even viewed it as "his thing." The way he saw it, he had to wear a shirt and tie all day at work, but

SHELTON H. SMITH JR.

his free time was his own, and he was going to enjoy it, loosen up, and let the good times roll!

Tommy was also a pretty active guy. He played basketball at the local gym a couple of times during the week, and in the summer months, he would rent a jet ski. He even tried his hand at surfing (but that didn't go so well, so he eventually crossed that off his list of activities). For Tommy, it wasn't about being good at everything—it was all about having fun. His active lifestyle gave him a rush, but he was about to realize that, much like a surfboard, life can move drastically and turn unexpectedly.

It was about two years ago when Tommy first began having stomach pain. At the time, he didn't think much of it. After all, he'd always pushed through any soreness or weakness, and it never stayed around long. He always said, "Tough it out. Don't let it beat you." Tommy truly believed that no sore muscle or common cold would ever knock him off his feet. He had way too much to do. With that in mind, Tommy pushed through that stomach pain, assuming that he must've eaten something bad or strained some sort of muscle. He just knew it would go away soon.

But it didn't. In fact, it got worse.

After a while, Tommy noticed that, along with the pain in his stomach, he was becoming tired on a regular basis. It was all he could do to make it through the workday, and after work, he just wanted to come home and flop on the bed. No longer did he have the strength or desire to do the things he loved. He didn't care to party or hang out with the guys anymore. All he had enough energy to do was go home and go to bed.

Things would continue to spiral downward for Tommy. Nothing he ate would stay down. He started missing a lot of days at work. His nightlife was dull and void. He was rapidly losing weight so quickly that he'd walk past a mirror and barely recognize himself. As if that wasn't bad enough, his mental state was declining. For Tommy, it seemed like everything was slowly slipping away.

Finally, Tommy couldn't take it anymore and decided to go see a doctor—something highly unusual for him. He had always been so strong and able to push through what was ailing him, but not this time. Maybe, Tommy thought, the doctor could give him a simple prescription to knock out the illness, and all would be well.

He made an appointment and made his way to the physician's office a few days later. After looking him over, the doctor decided to run some tests to better understand what was going on. The results came back, and Tommy was referred to a specialist. The specialist ran even more tests and told Tommy that they would discuss the results in a week or so. By this point, Tommy was getting worried, and having to wait a week to learn what was happening to him was worse than the illness itself.

After what seemed like a very long time, the specialist called Tommy back in to discuss the results of his tests. *At long last,* Tommy thought, *questions will be answered!* He found himself somewhat excited and somewhat anxious on the ride back to the specialist's office. When he arrived, he parked his car, walked to the front door, and took a deep breath to relax.

Tommy didn't even get a chance to sit in the waiting room; the receptionist told him to go straight back to meet with the specialist. He did, a little hesitant at how quickly everything was happening, and found the specialist in his office. He politely greeted the specialist, closed the door, and took a seat. With an eager look on his face, Tommy stared at the specialist. After several uncomfortable, silent words, the specialist finally opened his mouth to speak. "Tommy, you have stomach cancer. We will have to operate as soon as possible."

Tommy's heart began to race. The color in the room seemed to turn gray, and he couldn't find any words to say. It was like he was in a dream. *Cancer is something other people have,* he thought. There was no way this was happening to him.

Except…it *was,* and this was the biggest hurdle he'd ever faced in his life.

The doctors moved quickly, and Tommy had the surgery just two days after learning he had stomach cancer. It all happened so fast that Tommy felt like he was still dreaming through everything. He had never been in a hospital in his entire life.

When he woke up from the surgery, he was in a hospital room, and doctors and nurses were standing over him. He still felt sick to his stomach, but the peace of mind that the cancer had been removed was very comforting. He looked up to see one of the doctors asking everyone else in the room to step outside. And in a matter of seconds, it was just Tommy and one doctor. That doctor then said a lot of things to Tommy, much of which was challenging to comprehend so fresh out of surgery. However, Tommy heard one sentence very clearly: "We did what we could, but unfortunately, the cancer has spread to other organs. You're going to need radiation and chemotherapy."

Another crushing, frightening blow to a man who had never been seriously ill in his life. The news would get even worse—the doctor told him that the chemotherapy and radiation wouldn't be a solution, but merely an *extension*. In fact, the treatments would only give Tommy another two to five years of life. Without those treatments, the doctor said, Tommy had six months to live at best.

Tommy felt like crawling through the floor. His entire world just came crashing down, and his mind quickly filled with the things he'd never get the chance to do. It just wasn't *fair*. Just a few short weeks ago, Tommy was leading the life of a vibrant young man! He had the world to gain and nothing to lose. It was so hard to believe that his awesome life would be over in as little as two years.

Over the next few days, Tommy didn't know what was worse: the sickness or the depression. So many doctors were constantly in and out of his hospital room, day in and day out. He just wanted to scream, but at the same time, he didn't want to be alone. There were times when Tommy didn't know what he wanted at all.

During one of those times when he was at his lowest, Julie walked in. She wasn't a nurse or a doctor, Tommy would learn. Julie was the hospital chaplain. Initially, Tommy wasn't too excited to learn that; he expected her to deliver some fiery words about hell and sinners. Tommy really wasn't in the mood to be preached at.

But Julie was different. She listened to Tommy: his hurt, his anger, his sorrow, his grief. She told him that he had a right to his own feelings, and that God understood. She said that God knew his pain because His son suffered much pain too. Up until then, Tommy had never really thought of it like that, but he realized that Julie was right. Jesus suffered then, and thousands of years later, Tommy had to undergo his own suffering. What Julie taught him next really opened his eyes; she said that God *fixed it* for Jesus then, and if Tommy accepted Him into his heart, He would fix it for him too.

Julie's words made sense to Tommy. A lot of sense. Tommy knew there was nothing more he could do to fix his problem, and the doctors only offered a temporary solution. In fact, Tommy realized, *everyone's* life is temporary when it all boils down. Nothing on earth lasts forever, but God can give eternal life. God gives eternal peace, eternal love, and eternal joy. Tommy's life may have hit rock bottom, but there's nothing too hard for God.

So, with Julie holding his hand, Tommy gave his life to God.

Today, Tommy is still undergoing chemotherapy treatments. It's not always easy, but his outlook on life is so much better. He has a new joy, a new peace, and a new hope for tomorrow. Of all the things he once valued—his job, the partying, the friends, the women, the activities—none of it matters anymore. He's just thankful to be alive, and he knows it's all because of God that everything has changed.

Tommy is at peace with himself and the world, and that peace didn't come when Tommy thought he was dreaming; instead, it came when God finally woke him up.

Sarah's Journey

Looking back over her life, it seemed like times were always hard for Sarah, just one struggle after another. Things she depended on constantly let her down, people she trusted in always came up short, and often, when she was just about to gain her footing again, her platform would collapse. Little by little, she found herself backing away from people because for her, "love" always ended in pain. She found it difficult to put trust or hope in anything because that vulnerability always seemed to backfire. At times, she felt she was searching for something, something that she would never find.

Even in her early years, she dealt with immense pain. Her parents hardly ever seemed to get along, starting one argument after another. Sometimes, her father would leave the home for days at a time, but it almost didn't matter. Regardless of his presence in the home, there was never any peace there. When he finally did return to the house, the fussing and bickering would immediately begin again.

Sarah can recall some good times here and there as she grew up, but even most of those occurred when her father wasn't at home. She remembers her parents as good people overall, and she loved them both, but she just didn't think they were good for each other.

Then one day, everything changed for Sarah; her life started to take a downward spiral. She was in the fourth grade, and her teacher informed her that she needed to report to the principal's office. Sarah got up and walked past her teacher's desk, but on her way to the door, she noticed a very odd look on her teacher's face. After pausing a moment, she decided it was nothing and proceeded to the hallway.

When she arrived at the principal's office, she was surprised (and a little excited) to see her mother and her father's brother, George. But then, Sarah surveyed the room and saw that they were seated in the office with the principal...and the school nurse. Suddenly, her happiness changed to uneasiness as the gloomy atmosphere in the room overcame her. She began to notice the sad expression on everyone's face, and her mother was wiping her face with a tissue. Sarah's uncle, George, then stood up and softly took her hand.

"Baby, we got some bad news today," he said to Sarah in a quiet, low voice. "Your daddy had a bad accident at work today. Some heavy equipment fell on him at the construction site, and they took him to the hospital..." Uncle George paused a moment as he stared into Sarah's wide eyes, waiting for her to say anything at all. When she didn't, Uncle George gulped and whispered, "but he didn't make it."

Sarah wanted to scream, but she couldn't. It was like her breath had been taken away. Her heart began racing, and the world around her seemed to slowly lose color. The weight of knowing she'd never speak to her father again sunk into her stomach, like an anchor to the bottom of the sea. The man she had waited for a deeper relationship with for so long was gone forever. She felt horribly sick...and empty.

A short time after the funeral, Sarah's mother started drinking alcohol heavily. At first, she told Sarah it was only to help her sleep. A few weeks later, she began to drink in the morning, claiming the cup or two was a "pick-me-up." Not much later, her mother was drinking several times a day on average. When Sarah questioned her about it, she said it was no big deal, and a drink here and there simply helped the day to pass.

But Sarah was noticing a significant change in her mom's personality. She began to be less pleasant and sociable, miss work on a regular basis, and stop hanging out with her girlfriends. Her mother was literally pulling away from life...and away from Sarah.

By age fifteen, Sarah felt like an orphan. Her father was gone, and her mother was an alcoholic. She found herself thinking, *Well, if I can't get love and attention at home, I'll get it somewhere else.* Shortly thereafter, she met a boy. And then another. And another. Eventually, Sarah gave herself to any guy who gave her as much as a passing glance, yearning desperately to fill the void in her heart. She was easily won over by anyone who told her she was pretty, would give them anything they want, and ask for nothing in return. She wasn't looking for commitment; she just wanted to feel love, even if only for a fleeting moment.

In spite of her circumstances, one positive element of Sarah's life was her schoolwork. She miraculously kept her grades up during these trying times and ultimately graduated from high school. Then she lost her momentum and directed her focus on the wrong things. Sarah's summer after high school graduation was filled with men, parties, and drug use. In her mind, it was her only source of happiness. Although that lifestyle was fun for a while, it wasn't who Sarah really was. She was only looking to fill the hole in her heart left by the absence of her parents, and the temporary excitement from her wild endeavors was not doing the job.

At age twenty-six, Sarah lost her mother to pancreatic cancer, and Sarah's outlook on life went from bad to treacherous. Over the next year or so, Sarah continued to party and sleep around, no longer because it gave her momentary joy, but because she felt she was too far gone to change. She became pregnant—twice—miscarrying each time. Extreme depression and withdrawal soon followed; although she didn't really want to be a mom, she was looking forward to possibly having someone unconditionally love her.

After the second miscarriage, Sarah was basically existing instead of living. She was walking down the street one day and happened to run into an old friend from middle school. They started talking, and Sarah's friend began to tell her about this dramatic change that just occurred in her life. She, much like Sarah, had gotten caught in the party scene but only found brief satisfaction. But one day, Sarah's friend visited a local church and gave her life to God.

She was speaking so quickly and excitedly that Sarah could barely keep up with what she was saying, but what was unmistakable was the way her friend's eyes lit up when she talked about her new life in Christ. She then invited Sarah to go to church with her that Sunday. Sarah was a little reluctant because she couldn't remember the last time she had been to a service, but her friend's joy was undeniable and something that Sarah could definitely use.

It wasn't until that Sunday when Sarah and her friend first arrived at morning service that she finally remembered the last time she had set foot in a church—her mother's funeral. Immediately, she became uncomfortable and started convincing herself that this whole thing was a bad idea.

Fortunately, though, Sarah's experience that day was nothing like the morning she laid her mother to rest. The people at the church service were warm and inviting, the music was lively and uplifting, and the preacher spoke of a God who loved everyone unconditionally. As someone who had spent the last several years looking for love, Sarah was all ears.

Listening to the pastor preach, a sense of peace fell over Sarah, and she immediately knew that it was the same peace her girlfriend had told her about a few days ago. It was the peace that Sarah had been missing for so many years and could never find.

At the end of the sermon, the pastor lifted his hands and said, "Anyone who desires the peace of God can have it." He then quoted John 3:16: "For God so loved the world, that He gave His only begotten Son, that whosoever believeth in Him, should not perish, but have everlasting life." After all of that, though, two words stuck out to Sarah: "peace" and "love." Sarah knew that if she didn't make a change, her life would continue to go nowhere fast. Up to that point, life had only offered her failure, disappointment, and broken promises.

The pastor officially invited the congregation to discipleship, and Sarah responded. She slowly made her way to the front of the church, accompanied by a roaring applause from those around her. And in that moment, Sarah realized she had found what she had always longed for. Love, joy, peace, and contentment had eluded her for so long; she couldn't find it in men, drugs, or partying. All that time, she had been looking in the wrong places. It was the love of Jesus that she had been searching for.

That day, Sarah not only accepted Jesus Christ as her Savior, but she became a member of that very church.

Fast forward a few years, and she is now active in several ministries and even sings in the choir!

The peace and love of God has taken over her troubled heart. What a miraculous change Jesus has made in her life.

Daniel's Comeback

Daniel had a pretty good childhood…about as good as anyone else's. He had a good home and good friends. As far as life went, his was all right. He played sports in school, and his grades were okay most of the time. Things went pretty well for him. He figured things would always go just the way they always had, but he would find out that circumstances don't always go as planned.

Daniel's home life was good. His mom worked part-time, and his dad drove trucks. His dad was gone most of the week, so his mom called him the "little man of the house." He filled in while his dad was away. He would help out around the house, and when his chores and schoolwork were done, he could go out and play with friends. When his dad would come home on the weekends, he would always bring home something for Daniel and his mom from whatever state he had to drive to. Daniel's mom would always fix a special dinner that night.

Daniel remembers a lot of good times growing up. As a child, his mom would read Bible stories to him before bed. They would say their prayers, and just before she turned his light out, she would always say, "Danny, trust in God, and do good." It became sort of a catch phrase for her. As Daniel got older, she would say it to him every morning before he left for school. Trust in God and do well. It's funny how things that seem so small and insignificant one day can be so powerful the next.

Daniel's dad had spent time in the navy. He was always telling Daniel of the times he spent on the ship, going different places around the world. He would tell of his old navy buddies and how much he enjoyed going to different ports and seeing different people. In a way, Daniel wanted to be just like him, so when he graduated, he joined the service. To be his own man, and do his own thing, Daniel joined the army. It gave him a sense of charting his own pathway in life.

Joining the army wasn't a fly-by-night decision for Daniel. He had plans. Big plans. He would stay in for twenty years, get a good college education while he was in, save his money, and after retirement, get a job in the technical field. He had it all worked out. Then he thought, *Well, maybe I'll start my own business when I get out.* The end result he wasn't quite sure about. "But no big deal," he figured. He had twenty years to work through that part.

It was during his second year in the army that his unit got deployed to Iraq. They were told that they would be there for six months if their orders didn't change. Getting that call was a little scary for Daniel, but he tried to keep his thoughts together by reminding himself, *This is what I've been training for.* They all knew their jobs, and their assignment was clear. They had good leadership, and as long as they followed orders, he'd be okay. *After all,* he thought, *this experience will just make me a better soldier and a better man. Every good soldier knows this day might come.*

Iraq's climate was very different from any he'd ever seen. It was a very dry heat. Every chance he got, he had to drink water to stay hydrated. It was a pretty miserable place, especially when there was a sandstorm. They had to protect their eyes and their noses because sand was blowing everywhere. When it was over, sand was everywhere in their clothes. Even their boots had sand in them. As hard as it was, it would soon get a whole lot worse.

One morning, a few of them were sent out on a routine patrol. They were sent out to cover this very mountainous terrain. Everything was going as planned until gunfire suddenly erupted. They all took what cover they could as mortar fire began to come at them. As they began to return fire, Daniel could hear the screams of his buddies crying out as they got hit. He had never been so scared in his whole life. It all seemed like a dream. A really bad dream.

They were pinned down for about three hours until another unit was able to join them. Even then, the shelling and the gunfire continued. Between firing off shots and trying to help the wounded, it was all Daniel could do not to lose his mind. With all the crazy thoughts going through his head, one thought rang out above all. It was his mother's voice. Daniel heard her say, "Trust in God, and do well." It was the one soothing thing in a chaotic situation. He began to pray, "Jesus, help me!" He tried to remember some old Bible verses but couldn't. He tried to remember some old choir songs but couldn't. The only thing he could remember was his mother's voice and her words, "Trust in God, and do good."

Some of the fellows got hurt that day, some pretty badly, but thankfully, no one lost their lives. There would be other patrols and other attacks by the enemy, but none as severe as that one. Daniel felt that God had really helped him out on that day, and he thanked Him for His help, but as time went on, he drew further away from God and closer to his old way of living, which meant for him to be strong and depend on himself.

Daniel had such big plans when he joined the army. He would stay in for twenty years, then get a good job. Well, sometimes, plans change. He had a motorcycle accident about a year and a half after returning from Iraq, and although he recovered, his leg was badly injured and never fully recovered. He was given a medical discharge and came home. He would soon find that his leg was not the worst of his problems. It was hard to find work coming home injured with no education and no skills. After a few months of trying, Daniel found himself becoming angry and somewhat bitter. *This is not the life I signed up for*, he told himself. *Everything is falling apart.*

About five months later, he got some more depressing news. One of his old high school buddies had died in a car accident. It seemed his once perfect life was going from bad to worse. Everything had been so clear at one point, and now everything in life was dark and cloudy.

When he went to the funeral, he was thinking, *God has really turned His back on me.* His life was going in a good direction, all his plans were laid out, his thoughts were together, and then everything changed—his horrifying army experience, his injury, coming home and not finding a job, and now he was sitting in the funeral of a good friend. Life couldn't be worse.

He was there for his friend, but all the while, he couldn't wait to get out of there. The whole service was a blur to him. He really wasn't paying attention until the preacher began to perform the eulogy. Daniel didn't remember his title, but he did remember that the pastor read from Psalm 31:3, "Trust in the Lord, and do good; so shalt thou dwell in the land, and verily thou shall be fed." His words rang out as if Daniel was the only one in the room. Trust in God and do good. That was what his mother had always told him. Those were the words that gave him comfort on the battlefield. It wasn't just an old saying from his mother. It was God's word.

All this time, Daniel was trying to make his own way. He was trusting in his own strength, but he found out his own strength wasn't good enough. He asked God to forgive his sin, and from then on, Daniel trusted in Him.

Two months after he gave his life to Jesus, he found a pretty good job. He even signed up for night classes in the fall. His life had a new direction: "Not my way, but God's way. Not my will Lord, but Thine be done." Jesus gave him what he couldn't get on his own.

Coming to Grips with Anger

Todd would say things had always gone pretty well for him. In school, he got pretty decent grades, was on the track team and the marching band, had some good times with his buddies, and did pretty well with the ladies. His home life was good too. His family had five kids, two boys and three girls. Todd was the second oldest. Overall, they were the average middle-class American family. His parents were hard workers who did their best to give them the essentials in life. They didn't get everything they wanted, but they got the things they needed.

Friday night at Todd's house was pizza, no cooking and no major cleaning, and Sunday was church day, Sunday school followed by morning service. Todd had a fairly close relationship with his parents, which was why he didn't get into too much trouble. During his senior year, Todd decided to apply to a college that was about a three-hour drive from home. It wasn't too far away, but far enough for him to get away and experience a new kind of existence. Upon hearing his plans, Todd's dad told him, "Todd, everything in your world is about to change. You won't have your family close, but always take God with you." Todd figured it was good advice. What else is a dad supposed to say?

In college, times were quite different from Todd's home life. His newfound freedom was great, and the responsibilities he learned growing up in a rather large household made it easier to deal with the responsibility of dorm life. Todd had friends, and he had fun. He followed his dad's advice—somewhat. He found a local church to attend, but he didn't go much. After having classes all week and living the college life on Saturday, it was just harder and harder to get up on Sunday.

It was during Todd's sophomore year that he met Julie. She was a cute little girl who sat in the front row of his science class. The first day that he saw her, he didn't hear much of what the teacher said. After class, he struck up a conversation, and before long, they were dating regularly. Of all the good college experiences Todd had, Julie was definitely the best.

They dated all through college. Julie was good to him and for him. She got Todd going to church on a regular basis again. Church was always a part of his life, but he had kind of gotten away from it. Their love for each other progressed over the years, and four years after graduation, when they both had decent jobs, they got married. Their lives were taking off in a very positive direction.

About a year and a half into their marriage, Todd woke up one morning to find Julie rather sick in the bathroom. He got up to help her out any way he could. He was thinking that she had a little virus or a stomach flu, so he offered to get her an aspirin or something else to make her feel better. However, she said that wasn't it. "Todd, I think I'm pregnant," she said. Pregnant! Todd was going to be a dad! His life was definitely an upward climb.

Nine months later, Julie gave birth to a baby girl: Taylor Joanne, six pounds, fifteen ounces. She was the most beautiful thing Todd had ever seen. It seemed to him that life was getting sweeter by the hour. He had his perfect little family. Taylor was fine, Julie was fine, and life was beautiful.

Two days later, Todd took his perfect little family home. His and Julie's families made the short trip to see the new grandchild. Everybody made a big fuss over the new baby, and Todd began to realize that in his parents' eyes, he had taken a backseat. The new grandchild came first. That was okay, however. He felt the same way.

Todd had always heard that the first baby is the toughest to deal with. That was certainly true for him. Nighttime feedings, diaper changes, doctor visits, and trying to figure out what Taylor needed when she cried was not only stressful, but it cost Todd and Julie a lot of sleep. To get through it, Todd kept telling himself, *This is what you asked for.* It seemed that he and Julie could never get enough rest. Still, when the baby was calm and the house was quiet, he was holding his precious bundle of joy. For these moments, it seemed like heaven on earth.

Taylor's crying kept Todd and Julie up every night, so they decided to take turns. First, Julie would get up, then Todd would. Taylor made sure there was enough getting up for everybody. Between late-night feedings and diaper changes, things seemed to be pretty lively all night long. Some of Todd's coworkers tried to comfort him by telling him that the older babies get, the longer they sleep. That was good news for the future.

November 15 was the day when things took an excruciating turn. It started off on a positive note. It was the first time in a long time that Todd was able to sleep through the night. He got up once to go to the bathroom, trying to keep as quiet as possible, so as not to wake the baby. When they both did get up, Julie commented that the baby must be getting older. "She's starting to sleep through the night," she said. As she went to check on Taylor, Todd went to take his shower and get ready for work. He was just about to brush his teeth when Julie let out the most awful, blood curling scream he had ever heard. Todd dropped everything, hoping to find that she had stubbed her toe or broken a dish, something insignificant like that. As he ran, though, he didn't even convince himself.

Todd followed the sounds to the baby's room. There was Julie, holding Taylor, screaming and crying, with a look of panic in her eyes. Todd grabbed his baby to find that she was cold and blue—lifeless. He tried to do CPR like they had been taught in the baby classes. Then he rushed to call 911, and the ambulance came and took Taylor.

When Todd and Julie got to the hospital, the doctor told them, "We did what we could, but there was nothing we could do." It was called sudden infant death syndrome (SIDS), crib death. It was nobody's fault. It just happened.

The grief was overwhelming and consuming. It was a torment that seemed unfair somehow. *Why did this happen?* Todd wondered.

How could it happen to me? I've always been a good guy. I treated people right. I went to church. Everything was going so well. Why would God let this happen?

Todd felt a bitterness in his spirit. He figured, *Well, if God can turn His back on me, I'll turn my back on Him.* He stopped going to church. He stopped going to Bible study. If God couldn't help him out, then Todd didn't need Him. He'd just live his life without Him.

Things began to get strained in their house. Julie wanted to go to church even more. She got more deeply involved in ministry and even started singing in the praise team. It seemed that Taylor's death drew her closer to God while it had the opposite effect on Todd. They seemed to argue over the smallest things now. It even made Todd angry to see her reading her Bible. He found himself developing a hate for her and everything she did. He even began to hate himself.

On one Wednesday night, when Julie was at church, Todd heard a ring at the front door. It was two of the deacons from church, the last people he wanted to see.

Todd said, "Julie's not here. I think she's at church."

They said, "We're not here for her, we're here for you."

Reluctantly, Todd invited them in. He figured that he'd let them talk for a while and get rid of them. They told him how much they missed him at church and how much they would like to see him get back involved because he was needed. Todd stumbled through a few excuses, made up some stories—basically anything to satisfy them.

It was about a half hour into the conversation that one of them said something that really stuck with him. The deacon said, "Todd, I know you're having a hard time with the loss of your beautiful baby, and maybe you're wondering why God let this happen to you. Well, Todd, maybe God is not angry with you, but maybe he knew you were the one guy who could handle it and give Him praise through it." That was an eye-opening thought. Maybe he hadn't been forgotten. Maybe he hadn't been done wrong. Maybe he was being used for God's glory.

But he still had all of this pain. This hurt. This sorrow. That's when the deacon quoted from 1 Peter 5:7, "Cast all your cares upon

Him, for he cares for you." Although he couldn't explain it, the verse gave Todd a sense of relief. A newfound joy began to creep into his heart. Todd hadn't been forsaken. He was chosen.

That day was a big turnaround for him. He and Julie began to get closer in their marriage and their Christian walk. They began to look at their lives as vessels that God used, and although they will never forget their little Taylor Joanne, God blessed them with three more children. God was able to turn tragedy into triumph.

A Father for Ron

At fourteen, Ron found himself with too much responsibility. He was the oldest with two younger brothers, and he had to focus much of his attention on them because their mother was in and out. Sometimes she was working, and sometimes she was God knows where. It had been like that for a long time because Ron's dad left a long time ago, and when he had, it seemed like everything changed. While Ron's childhood wasn't perfect, that was a major shift.

As a child, Ron's times with his dad were fun. They would watch TV, play board games, and go outside and throw the football around. Ron's dad wasn't around all the time. He was the kind of guy who worked hard...at not working. Oh, he bought their home, ran numbers, placed bets for people, sold drugs, and basically anything else that would get him some money. Ron knew that it wasn't the best way to make a living, but it didn't seem to matter to him because his father was good to him.

When Ron was nine, Ron's mother's attitude seemed a little different. She seemed quieter, less responsive. Ron also noticed that his dad hadn't been around for a few days. When he asked her about his dad, she told him, "He's gone, and I hope he never comes back." Ron was totally blown away. As she left the room, he did hear her mumble something about another woman. Ron thought to myself, *This can't be really happening*. Ron's dad was always gone for some time, but it was hard to believe that he'd never see him again.

Soon after that day, things began to change for them. It seemed that his mother's mind-set was to do her own thing and make a life for herself. She began hanging out at night and leaving Ron to deal with his two younger brothers. That was a lot for him to handle, but he did the best he could. Trying to calm their fears at night was difficult for him, seeing as though he was scared himself.

Sometimes, Ron's mother was out all night, which meant that he had to get everybody ready for school the next day, including himself. Even when she would make it home, she was too tired to get up in the morning with them. It really made for a tough time growing up. Ron started failing at his schoolwork. His grades began to slip. It seemed that whatever good he had in his young life was slowly slipping away. If only his dad were here, everything would be all right.

By the age of fourteen, Ron was completely stressed out. He had too much on his shoulders and no one to help him. Things weren't good at home or at school, but he did have friends—well, he called them friends. It was the local gang in his neighborhood. He started hanging out with them more and more. They made him feel better, feel safer. They had his back, and he had theirs. The gang became his new family. He hadn't felt this secure since his dad left.

About a year later, Ron and a couple of the guys decided to rob the corner market. He, Vince, and Freddy, the leader of the gang, had this plan: Freddy would go in and get the money from the cash register while he and Vince would grab all the food they could, mostly concentrating on pizza and beer, so they could go back and have a big party with the gang. Freddy carried a gun with him—a nine-millimeter. It was all set.

They went in at about eight-thirty at night. Freddy rushed to the counter for the money while Vince and Ron headed towards the big cases of beer. Ron's heart was racing. He was on an adrenaline rush. He would go for the beer, and Vince would grab some frozen pizzas. The plan was perfect.

Ron had just picked up two cases of beer and was headed toward the door when he heard the first pop. Then two more pops. Freddy was shooting. Something was going wrong. He wasn't supposed to shoot, just get the money and run. When Ron got to the front, he realized what was happening. It was a gunfight. Freddy and the store clerk were shooting at each other. Ron dropped everything and ducked behind the display cases. It was a mess, the worst situation he had ever been in. He just wanted to get out.

It seemed that Ron was behind that case hiding for a long time although it was probably really only a few seconds. He made a run for the door and heard another pop, but he made it out. He was outside, but he kept running. He didn't know if he was running from that clerk or the whole situation, but he just kept running. When he finally stopped about three blocks later, he was out of breath and soaked with sweat, partly because of the running, but mostly because of the fear. As he stood there, he really didn't know what to do with himself. Part of him wanted to go back and see about his friends, and part of him just wanted to go home. He decided on the latter.

It wasn't until the next day that Ron found out what happened. Freddy had been shot. It seemed the store clerk had a gun too, and that wasn't all he had. He had their description. They were in and out of that store all the time, and he remembered them. All three of them were arrested for armed robbery.

Being juveniles, they were sentenced to juvenile detention. It was kind of rough, but in the back of his mind, Ron knew it could be a lot worse in adult prison. In detention, they had counselors, people who tried to get them back on track. Ron resisted their counsel for a while, but little by little, he recognized that he did need to change. After all, he had two younger brothers. If nothing else, somebody had to be there for them.

They also had Christian counselors, people who would tell them about the love of God. It didn't mean much to Ron at first. The way he saw it, God had never meant much before—He certainly had never helped him before—so why would He help him now? Why would He care now? And for that matter, why should Ron care about Him?

God didn't mean too much to Ron until they described Him as a heavenly Father. That word stuck with him. Heavenly Father. Ron's own father had meant so much to him.

He hadn't been perfect, but he was good to Ron. Ron's family life was better when his dad was around. Ron's whole life and all that he had done was wrapped up in trying to fill the void that his dad left.

The counselor told Ron how much his heavenly Father loved him and had done so much for him. He told Ron that if he would give God his heart, then God would make Ron His son. Then he gave Ron a scripture from Romans 10:9: "If thou shalt confess with thy mouth the Lord Jesus, and shalt believe in thy heart that God hath raised Him from the dead, thou shalt be saved." This verse had a special meaning to Ron. God, the Father, wanted him to be His son, and Ron desperately wanted a father in his life.

Ron accepted Jesus as his Lord and Savior, and after all those years, he finally had a relationship with a father. Not only that, but God gave him a special gift. About one month after Ron got out of detention, they got a call that his dad wanted them to come see him. He had been sick, diagnosed with terminal cancer. They drove the two-hour trip to Mercy Hospital. When they got to his room, Ron was both happy and sad—happy to have his father again, but sad for his situation. Nevertheless, he composed himself, and he suddenly found himself witnessing about Jesus to his dad. To Ron's surprise, he accepted Jesus, right there in his hospital bed. For a long time, Ron had been acting out, searching for the love of his father, and then, by the grace of God, he had two.

The Blame Game

For the better part of her life, Annie really never liked to accept responsibility for her actions. She had always found, even at an early age, that it was better to avoid trouble than to accept it. She put more energy into getting out of trouble than standing up to it. She hated punishment, she hated restriction, and she hated missing out on a good time. While she recognized that it was fear and immaturity on her part, it was always easier to point fingers at somebody else than at herself. Whatever it was, it started her as a competitive athlete in the blame game.

No matter what mischief Annie found herself in, what got broken, or what she failed to accomplish, her first thought was to find a way to transfer the attention to one of her two sisters and one brother. It didn't always work, but oftentimes, it did. It was easy to pass the blame, and it kept her position as a "good child" intact. It worked for a while until her parents caught on, and she went from the "good child" to the "tattletale." Annie didn't care; by then, blame was in her blood.

Schoolwork was always a struggle for her. It wasn't that she couldn't do it, but her mind was always full of things she'd rather be doing. Instead of focusing on what was important, her mind would drift to what made her happy. Most of the time, Annie could pull it off and make the best of it. She usually got pretty decent grades in school, but not always. Her mother was always telling her, "Annie, you've got to keep your focus. You've got to pay attention in class." Of course, Annie always had an excuse for poor grades.

Math was always Annie's worst subject. One report card day, her worst fear came true. She had two Bs, three Cs, and a really big *F* in math. Annie was horrified. Her grades were never perfect, but she had never gotten a failing grade. That was the longest bus ride home in history. Annie didn't say two words to her friends on the bus because her full attention was on what she was going to say to her parents. The only thing that came to her mind was to rely on the familiar. She was going to put trust in her old ways.

By the time she got off the bus and made it up to her front porch, her plan was set. She would blame her bad grade on the teacher who had never liked her, would always fuss at her, and sometimes made Annie stand at the back of the lunch line for no reason at all. Annie assumed that would work. It certainly wasn't the grade she deserved. She should have gotten a *C*, or maybe a *B*. She probably could have made the honor roll if it hadn't been for her teacher hating her so much. Unfortunately, Annie's words fell on deaf ears, and she was grounded for a month.

That incident didn't cause Annie to change her ways. It only motivated her to be more creative in her blaming. Next time, she'd keep her cool so she could think better; next time, she wouldn't come up with something so obvious and juvenile; next time, she'd be better prepared.

About a week after she got off punishment, Annie was riding her bike home from a friend's house. Coming up the driveway, she got a little too close to her dad's car, and her handlebar scratched the door. It was a really bad one too. It not only took the paint off, but it left a little dent. To make matters even worse, Annie's dad had this thing about his car. He was always washing and waxing it. Before she could get in it, she had to change her shoes or wipe them off if they were muddy. Annie thought her dad was obsessed with his car. Whatever the case, it really didn't matter. She was in for it.

Of course, Annie's mind started racing. How was she going to get out of this? What was she going to say? She had to think of something. She thought for a while, and she soon came up with what she thought was the perfect story to tell her parents. Her brother, Joey, and his friends were always riding their bikes around the neighborhood. They were always wild and crazy, throwing footballs and knocking each other around. Surely her parents would believe that Joey would do something like this.

It felt good to have her plan worked out. It was kind of a relief to have everything figured out in her head. Nothing beats a good story—except an eyewitness. Annie's mom saw what she had done through the kitchen window. When Annie came in, she didn't say anything at first, and neither did Annie. She was just waiting for the right moment to tell her tale.

It wasn't until dinner that the scratch came up. Annie's mom said in a firm but cool voice with one eyebrow raised, "Your dad's car was scratched today. I believe one of you kids knows how it got there."

Immediately, Annie blurted out, "It must have been Joey! You know how wild he and his friends can be."

Of course, her words started a big argument between her and Joey, but their mom quickly put a stop to it by simply saying, "Annie, I saw you do it." Busted! A testimony from an eyewitness will get you the electric chair every time.

One might think that Annie would have learned her lesson by then, but old habits are hard to break. Years later, she got a part-time job as a waitress while taking college courses at night. She really enjoyed her job. Her coworkers were pleasant, and there was a friendly group of regular customers. Still, whenever something wasn't put back in its proper place or an order was given to the cook wrong or a spill wasn't cleaned up fast enough, someone else got the blame. It started to cause some tension between Annie and her coworkers, but she figured, *So what? As long as I get my paycheck, it doesn't matter.*

One day, as it was getting close to quitting time, Annie was washing her hands at the sink. She noticed that someone had left one of those Christian church tracks lying on the counter. She never had much use for church, although her family went every now and then. Still, this little pamphlet caught her eye, probably because of all the bright colors and nice artwork, and she picked it up and took it with her.

When Annie got home, she read through it. It had an interesting storyline. It was about a guy who lived his life just the way he wanted to, did whatever made him happy. He worked, he partied, he traveled; he did everything to please himself. But one day, he died in a motorcycle accident, and his soul went to hell with no chance of ever getting out.

At that point, the little comic book didn't seem so funny anymore. It seemed real. Maybe it was real. This guy seemed like a pretty good guy, but he went to hell. Annie had always thought that only bad people went to hell.

The last page told her why he went to hell. It explained everything about his life, and it shed light on her own. It quoted 1 Corinthians 1:7–8: "So that ye come behind in no gift, waiting for the coming of our Lord Jesus Christ: Who shall also confirm you unto the end, that you may be blameless in the day of our Lord Jesus Christ."

Blameless—that word stuck with her. All her life, Annie had blamed everybody else for things she had done, and sometimes she had gotten away with it. Still, the blame for her own wrongdoings was really hers, and God knew it. However, Jesus was offering to take it away!

Then Annie read another scripture in that pamphlet. Isaiah 28:15: "We have made lies our refuge, and under falsehood have we hid ourselves." That really hit home. It was like the Bible was talking directly to her. Lies and falsehoods had been a refuge for her. A hiding place. Lies and falsehoods were a way for her to stay out of trouble but would ultimately lead to her destruction.

The track went on to answer the questions Annie had in her mind and gave her the perfect answer to her distorted life.

First John 1:9 reads, "If we confess our sins, He is faithful and just to forgive our sins and cleanse us from all unrighteousness."

That was Annie in a nutshell. She was blaming everybody else for her wrong. She'd spent her whole life pointing the finger at others. For the first time in her life, Annie took responsibility for her life. Her sins were her own.

She bowed her head and asked Jesus to take her sin, clean her up, and make her new.

Suddenly, she felt a release like a weight had been lifted. She immediately knew that Jesus had accepted her and would help her live a new life as a Christian. No more sin, no more sorrow, and no more blame. The blame game was over. Jesus set her free.

The Green-eyed Monster
Meets the Holy Ghost

Terry thinks that God may have had his hands full trying to save her. They say that Jesus's blood is sufficient for salvation, but Terry believes that her case required a little extra blood.

She wasn't a drug dealer or a prostitute—nothing like that. Her sin was a little subtler, a little less obvious. It was the type of sin that most people overlook. She did. People overlook it because everybody has to deal with it every once in a while. It's just that, for Terry, it had her consumed. It was something she couldn't escape, and at times she really didn't want to. When her sin got hot, it burned like a forest fire. Her sin, quite frankly, had her seeing green!

Terry doesn't remember too many things about her childhood. Everything went fairly well for her family. They lived in a nice neighborhood, they had a big four-bedroom house with a big backyard, they had a swimming pool, and she had her own jungle gym. In the summer, they would take a vacation in the mountains, take cruises, and go to theme parks. Her parents owned a furniture business and worked hard throughout the year, so when they needed a break, they always did it up big. Because of the family wealth, Terry seemed to get everything she wanted. She always had the latest toys, the finest clothes—you know, the best of everything. Life for this only child wasn't bad at all. For most little girls, growing up the way she did would have been a dream. It was for her—most of the time—but quite often, she had the feeling that enough was never enough.

As said before, everything Terry had growing up was the best—the most expensive, top of the line—and all the kids knew it. She

37

had the best bicycle of all her friends. It was lime green with a white seat, curved handlebars, and three speeds. All her girlfriends loved to ride on it; even some of the boys wanted to take it for a spin. They all loved it, and so did she.

One Saturday afternoon, Terry was headed to her friend's house for her tenth birthday party. It was just up the block from her house, so she rode her bike.

They had a wonderful time at the party. There was a clown who put on a magic show, they made balloon animals, had face painting, and played party games. When all that was done, they sang happy birthday and ate cake and ice cream. Then it was time to open the presents. There were clothes, shoes, toys, and video games—all really nice stuff. Terry's friend was so excited, and Terry was really happy for her. That is, until she got the last gift. It was a bicycle, fire engine red, with silver handlebars, and ten speeds. A ten-speed bike! All the kids made such a fuss over it. One girl said, "That's the coolest bike I've ever seen!" Somebody else said, "It's the best one in the whole neighborhood." It immediately became clear that Terry was no longer the head of the bicycle department. It left her feeling like she was onstage, and her spotlight went out while her friend began to shine even brighter.

Terry hated that feeling. She hated her friend for the attention she got. She hated the bicycle, and what's worse, she began to hate her friend. They had been friends for a long time, but every time Terry saw her on that bike, it made her angrier and angrier. After a while, Terry even hated her without the bike, and she didn't mind letting her know it either. She would roll her eyes at her, make little remarks to hurt her feelings, and even say things about her behind her back. Terry thought to herself, *Who does she think she is, anyway? She's just trying to be better than everybody else with that stupid bike. I'll fix her. I'll just get a better bike.* But Terry's parents said no; the one she had was still good. It made Terry hate her friend even more.

This was not an isolated incident of jealousy for her. Because of the "privileged" attitude that she had developed, it seemed she never could stand to see someone have something that she wanted.

Another episode of jealousy that stood out was in high school. Jerrod Perry was captain of the football team. He was tall, muscular, and had his own car. Whenever he came around, all the girls would speak to him in hopes that he would show them a little recognition. They all couldn't help but give him their undivided attention when he walked by. But all of his attention was focused on Patty Holly. Patty was a girl with a medium build and long red hair who sat in the second row of Terry's science class. They dated for a while and became a couple. Now, Terry didn't think Patty was ugly or anything. She was okay looking, sort of, but Terry really didn't get it. It made her sick every time Patty walked into that classroom. "How come she gets Jerrod? What's so special about her?" All the girls hated Patty. Well, Terry did.

A year later, it was Terry's senior year in high school. Everybody was hustling and bustling, getting ready for graduation and putting in applications to different colleges. Terry's future plans were already set. Both her parents were graduates of NC State, and she had already secured arrangements to attend there in the fall. While everybody else was so nervous about what college would accept them, it felt good to let everybody know that her plans were already in place. When the acceptance letters started arriving, people began to reveal where they would be attending college. Some were going to the local university, and some were going out of state. A few of the kids got some small scholarships to help pay tuition while others were quickly turning in financial-aid forms. One girl in their graduating class got a full four-year scholarship to Princeton. Terry didn't know her personally, but she figured she must be some nerd with no social life.

A couple of months from graduation, everyone was excited again. They were finally going to get out of high school. High school was a wonderful experience for Terry. Her grades were always pretty good, a few As, but mostly Bs and Cs. All the graduates were told to meet in the gym after school to pick up their cap and gown. Terry went after school, and when she gave them her name, they gave her a cap and gown with tassel that had the school colors, red and white. This was fine until she noticed the gold tassels and shawls that some of the students were getting. That gold really stood out against the black robes the others were wearing. Once again, that old green-eyed monster rose up in her. *Those kids weren't anything special,* Terry thought. *Why should they stand out? I think the administrators were playing favorites.*

That summer, much of Terry's time was spent getting ready for college in about a month or so. Most of her focus was buying matching outfits and shoes, the important stuff. She could get the school supplies when she got to campus and got settled in. One particularly boring afternoon, while her parents were working, and all her friends were out somewhere doing whatever, Terry decided to sit down and watch a little TV. Flicking through the guide, she thought to herself, *Over four hundred channels, and nothing's on that's interesting.* She came to one of those TV preachers, talking about the Ten Commandments. Terry figured she'd stop and listen to her for a while, because she wanted, like any good student, to see how many she was getting right. The preacher talked about honoring God. *Well,* Terry thought, *I'm nice. I guess that's the same thing.* The preacher talked about not having grown images and worshiping them. Terry certainly didn't do that. The preacher talked about taking the Lord's name in vain. Okay, Terry blew that one. Then came "Thou shalt not steal and Thou shalt not kill." Terry had never stolen anything or killed anyone; she was pretty good there.

On most of the commandments, Terry thought she was getting a failing grade. Some she never did, and some she was flunking out big time. Then the preacher got to "Thou shalt not covet." At first, Terry didn't know what that meant. Then the preacher explained that it means to want something that someone else has to the point of being jealous. KABOOM! That one sunk Terry's battleship. That one hit her like a ton of bricks. It was almost as if that was meant just for her. She wanted to turn the channel, but she had to keep listening. Maybe the preacher would say something else to make her feel better.

Terry kept watching until the preacher was finished. The more the preacher talked, the more unredeemed Terry felt. All this time she figured that her life was above average, but according to this preacher, she had only been fooling herself.

Near the end of the program, the preacher said, "If you've failed at any of these commandments, remember, God doesn't hate you. He hates what you did. God loves you enough to send His Son to die for your sin, and if you accept Jesus dying for your sin, you shall be saved." Those words went from Terry's ears directly to her heart. She accepted Jesus as her Lord and Savior that afternoon.

Ever since that day, Terry's life has taken a dramatic turn. She can now be happy for other people because she has the joy of the Lord as her strength. She thanks God that He gave her the Holy Ghost to chase away the green-eyed monster.

Joy Finds Real Joy

Joy was always raised to help people. She, her brother, and her parents were always involved in some charity or project to help out the less fortunate. Lifting up their fellow man gave them a sense of peace and tranquility. It was fulfilling and satisfying, and even at an early age, Joy and her brother always looked forward to the next event. Their dad used to tell them all the time, "Getting something is good, but giving back is so much better." For Joy, those were words to live by, and while she still felt that giving back is important, it became clear to her that all her giving would never come close to the gift that had been offered to her through God's Son. Life gave Joy peace and contentment, but Jesus gave her real joy.

Joy's parents were always charitable people, even before they got married. In fact, that's how they met. After college, they both worked for an organization that raised money to send food and medical supplies to needy countries overseas. They met, and after eight months of dating, got married. A couple of years later, her brother, Joseph, was born, followed by her three years later. Joy and her brother followed in what one might call the family footsteps. Her parents loved to serve, and they always kept them involved.

Joy's mom's favorite thing to do was the clothing drives. She, a few of her friends, and Joy were always collecting clothes from people that were still in good condition, and at the end of the week, they would take them down to the homeless shelters, the women's shelter, or a church charity. Joy would never miss a time to go with her mom and the other ladies because she enjoyed seeing the looks on the people's faces. It gave her a warm feeling inside, like she was doing something good. She even felt, "I guess I must be a good person for doing it."

Every year, Joy's dad and Joey would participate in a father-and-son golf tournament that raised funds for the local children's hospital. Her dad was a fairly decent golfer. He had been playing for several years. Joey didn't play; he just went along as her dad's caddy. After the game, the men would go out to a nice dinner, and of course, exaggerate their scores to each other. It all made for a fun day for a worthy cause.

At Christmas time, Joy's family, along with some others, would always get together and sing Christmas carols at the nursing home. All of these people were elderly, sick, or mentally challenged. Many of them didn't have families, or their family rarely came to see them. They would sing in the dining area, and the residents were always so excited. They would even sing along. Then at the end, they would pass out some small gifts to each of the residents, and then they would go and sing to the ones who were bedridden. After leaving the nursing home on those evenings, it always gave Joy a sense of pride that she had done something nice for someone in need.

As Joy got older, she acquired a job in a management firm. The hours were long sometimes, but she enjoyed the work, and she really had some awesome coworkers. One really good thing about her job is that it left her weekends free for her passion, volunteering. By this time, Joy was out at a local soup kitchen. For four hours on Saturday and Sunday, she would help prepare soup for the homeless, serve it, and help clean up. It was a lot of work, but it felt good to give back, like her dad had always said. None of them were rich folk, but Joy's way of thinking was, "When you give from your heart, it shows how big your heart is."

One Sunday morning, when Joy was working the soup line, one of the homeless men got his soup and his bread, then looked her in the eye and said, "I thank my God for people like you."

His words were kind of disturbing. They threw her off somehow. She said to him, "No need to thank God. Thank the homeless organization for the food. They're the ones that did it."

SHELTON H. SMITH JR.

He looked a little puzzled. "You're not a Christian?" he asked.

"I don't need a God when I can take care of myself!" Joy snapped back.

Then as he was walking away, he simply said, "I'm going to pray for you."

Joy was shocked and a little offended. Here she was, trying to help these homeless people, and this guy thought she needed his prayers. Well, she didn't need his prayers. She didn't need his God. She could do fine by herself.

The next week, Joy was back on the serving line, and there was the same homeless guy. Joy thought to herself, *I'll get him first before he gets me.* As he came through the line, she said to him, "Are you back again? If there was a God, seems like He would have given you your own house by now."

His answer came quickly, "I'm back because there is a God. He's supplying my need for food. God gave me these clothes to wear and a place to stay. All without having a job. So many people didn't wake up this morning. But I'm still alive, only by the grace of God!" He ended his words by saying, "I'm still praying for you."

When all the people finished eating, and they headed for the door, Joy made it her business to say one last word to that guy before he left. She met him right before he got to the door and said to him, "You're a mighty cheerful guy, not to have much."

His answer was simple and direct. "I've got Jesus, and that's enough. And one day, when this life is over, I'll live with him in heaven, forever."

Joy had never thought too much about heaven, and she had really never thought about dying, but now, she couldn't seem to stop thinking about either one. "People die all the time, and one day, I guess it will be my turn. What really happens when you die? Where do you go? Is there nothing else? Is there a heaven? Is there a hell?" Joy began to have so many questions and not a single answer for any of them.

Eventually, she got to the point where she looked forward to seeing that homeless guy, basically because he seemed to have answers to all these new questions that were swirling around in her head. His name was John, and he once owned a car mechanic business, but due to the economy, he lost it. With no money coming in, he lost his home, but with all that he lost, he never lost his faith in God. He was trusting God to someday get him back on his feet.

Talking to John gave Joy comfort in a way, but it also made her uncomfortable because she didn't have that same peace he had for the future. She didn't have the same rest in her soul. Her thoughts began to bounce between staying in her old comfortable life and turning to this God that John knew.

About three weeks later, as she was still wrestling with all these thoughts, she got a startling phone call from her mother. Her brother, Joseph, was in a construction accident at work. Joy was frantic. Her family had always been close. Her mind was already unsettled, thinking about how to fix her own life, and now this. Her mom assured her that even though he had a broken leg, bruised ribs, and would be laid up for a while, Joseph would be okay.

Her words calmed Joy down, but she still had her mind made up to meet the family at the hospital to be by her brother's side.

On the way, she thought about how fast things can happen and how fragile life really is. Her thoughts went from Joseph to herself. She needed answers to the questions of life. She needed to be sure of her own afterlife. She needed the peace that the homeless man had. She needed Jesus.

Right there in her car on the interstate, she prayed, "Lord, if you'll have me, I'm ready to accept you as my Savior." Immediately, she felt at peace. Immediately, she felt God's love. It was as soothing and comforting as a warm sweater, fresh from the dryer.

Joy is still volunteering and still doing what she can to help people. The difference is that she's not doing it to feel good anymore. Now, she wants to help people because of the love of God. Now, she does it because Jesus gave His joy to Joy's heart.

A Brand-new Jacob

Jacob always knew from a very early age that God had a plan for his life. It was really never hard for him to believe in a higher power because he was very young and ready and willing to receive, as most young kids are, anything that adult role model would tell him. He thanks his God so much for a Christian grandmother, as well as other church leaders, that took the time to tell him about the love of God—a God who created him and even knew him before he was born. He also gives praise to Jesus; not only did He save Jacob at the tender age of seven, but He began to use him in His redemption plan for Jacob's family. His name is Jacob, just like that guy in the Old Testament. He kind of identifies with him too. God used Jacob in the Bible to bless his family, and that's just what God did with him.

Every summer, when Jacob was little, his grandma would take him and his little brother to a vacation Bible school at their church. They also went to church with her on Sunday because they stayed with her on weekends. Jacob and his brother always looked forward to going to their grandma's house. She had a big backyard with a swing set and a slide, and while they were playing, she would always bake something. Cookies, pies, cupcakes. Their grandma always had the best smelling house in town. At night before bed, she always read them a bedtime story from the Bible. On Sunday, they went to Sunday school and church. That was Jacob's weekend. It was good for him and his brother, and it was good for his parents. They never went to church, and they enjoyed doing their own thing with the kids out of the house for the weekend.

One weekend at Grandma's house, Jacob asked her a question that had puzzled him for some time. He asked, "Grandma, how come Mom and Dad don't go to church?"

Her answer was quick and simple. "We need to pray that God will make them want to go." So they did, right there in the living room. They prayed that God would make Jacob's folks want to come to church. It made him feel pretty good. He had just prayed for God to save his parents. It also made him feel bold. When his little brother walked in the room, Jacob turned to him and said, "Toby, do you know Jesus?"

He answered, "Huh?"

Jacob asked him again, "Do you know Jesus?"

He said, "No."

Jacob said, "Do you want to know him?"

He said, "Uh, yeah."

Jacob then said, "Do you want Jesus Christ as your Savior?"

He said, "Yeah."

Jacob said to him, "I'm going to pray that Jesus will save you."

He said, "Okay."

So they held hands and prayed for Toby's salvation. At the end of the prayer, Jacob told him, "And now you're saved."

He said, "Okay."

It felt really good to get his brother saved, and it was really easy—probably because Toby was only four.

Jacob's parents, however, would prove to be a lot more difficult. For a long time, possibly about three years, nothing changed with them. Jacob and Toby spent the weekend at their grandma's house, and their parents did whatever they wanted with the free time. Then one evening after dinner, Jacob's mom told him and his brother that she had gotten laid off her job. It was something about the economy, and the company was not doing as well as they once had, but she assured them that there was nothing to worry about. Everything would be fine. Jacob thought to himself, *Her words sound one way, but her face tells a different story.*

Jacob's suspicions were correct. With less money coming in, things got pretty tight around the house. His family had to cut back on many of the things they had grown accustomed to, but that wasn't the worst part. His parents began to argue with each other more and more. At first, they tried to keep their voices down when Jacob and his brother were around. After a while, even that changed. They would scream at the top of their voices with the boys in the room. During this time, it was not only a pleasure but a relief to get to their grandma's house. This whole situation didn't make sense to Jacob. He had prayed to God for his family to get better. Instead, the family seemed to deteriorate.

It was pretty stressful during this time with the lack of money coupled with all the arguing, but they were making it with one paycheck. That is, until Jacob's dad suffered a back injury on his welding job at the shipyard and had to go on disability. That's when things around the house really started to get desperate. There never seemed to be enough of anything, and the arguments got louder and more intense. It got to the point that when Jacob did go outside to play, he dreaded coming back into the house. He finally came to the conclusion that it must be his fault. He must have done something bad. He had prayed that God would make his family better, but because of whatever he had done wrong, God was doing the exact opposite. Jacob wished that he had never prayed that stupid prayer.

The arguing and the yelling seemed to go on for months. Eventually, Jacob's dad left the house. He was devastated. Where was his dad going? Where would he live? Would Jacob ever see him again? He was totally heartbroken.

It did make things a lot quieter in the house, but not in a good way. Jacob's mom seemed sad all the time, but she tried to keep a brave face for Jacob and Toby. That lasted for some time.

Then one day, Jacob saw her on the sofa, and she looked like she had been crying. When he asked her what was wrong, she said, "Well, Jacob, you're a big boy now, and I can't keep it from you any longer. I went to the doctor last week, and he told me that I have melanoma, skin cancer." Jacob felt like the whole world was caving in around him, and there was nothing he could do about it. He prayed to God that he would forgive him for whatever he did to make Him so mad. Jacob's mom needed God's help. His dad needed God's help.

All of them needed God's help. This may have been the weirdest and most confusing time of Jacob's life. He was sliding between moments of total faith in God and moments of total rejection.

Jacob's mom started her cancer treatments, and after a few weeks, her attitude started improving. She had some more treatments to go, but her doctor told her things were going well. That weekend, Jacob and his brother were once again at Grandma's. On that Sunday morning, the doorbell rang. It was Jacob's mom and her sister, Mary. They said they wanted to go to church with them.

"Really?" This was amazing. Jacob didn't even see this coming. It almost seemed like a dream. The whole family was going to church. Could it be that God was starting to like Jacob again?

If that wasn't enough, Jacob's mom and aunt Mary both rededicated their lives back to the Lord. It seemed Mom and Aunt Mary had both gotten saved in their younger days, but when they grew up, they left the church. Now they were making a decision to come back to Christ. This was awesome!

Things got even better. Jacob's parents reconciled. His dad's back had gotten better, he'd found a new job, and wanted to come back home. He even went to church with them and eventually got saved. Then it dawned on Jacob. God was never mad at him. He had answered his first prayer. God used all that had happened to Jacob's family to draw his parents closer to Him. Jacob didn't understand it, but God knew what He was doing. He had a pretty good plan from the start. Jacob sort of is like Jacob in the Bible. They've got the same name, and God used them both to bless their families. Jacob truly is brand-new.

Arrested and Sentenced to Freedom

Life had always been a challenge for Pete. Growing up on the wrong side of the tracks was tough. It seemed like his family never had enough—never enough food, never enough clothes, never enough of anything—and they were always moving. No one let them stay in an apartment long since they didn't pay their bills. Even when they stayed with relatives, it wasn't too long. That had to do with money too. Moving from place to place sort of made Pete feel like nothing was permanent. Homes weren't permanent. It kind of made him a little hard, a little less caring. It certainly made him grow up fast. He felt like he had to do things for himself because he couldn't depend on anybody else. Nobody and nothing was going to look out for him, except him. That was Pete's motto back then…but now, he's got a new one, and that is: "God can fix a life that you didn't even know was broken!"

As a young teenager, Pete found that crime came pretty easily to him. His first crime was simple: snatching purses from old ladies. He would come up behind them, grab the purse, and start running. Talk about a major adrenaline rush. Each time was more exciting than the last. It wasn't extremely profitable though. One time, he did get sixty-two dollars, but mostly, he got between ten and twenty-five. A few times, he just got a bag full of junk, but it didn't bother him too much. To Pete, the reward was good, but the thrill ride was even better.

Stealing purses was fun and exciting, but Pete didn't stay there. He realized that a good way to make money was to steal expensive items and sell them on the street, so he and a couple of buddies started breaking into nice homes. They would get all kinds of stuff: TVs, computers, electronics, jewelry, and watches. No sooner than they would get them, they'd sell them and start counting up the money. It was awesome—an even better ride than those purses.

Of course, for Pete, even this wasn't enough. He had started using drugs about a couple of years before this. Nothing big, just marijuana. At about this time, his dealer said to him, "Every week you give me your money. Along with that, how about making us some money?" His plan sounded pretty good to Pete. He could sell dope, along with stolen property, and make more money than ever. Some might say that his life was on the upswing, but actually, things were spiraling out of control.

Pete's career of crime flowed like a river for a while. His drug business was expanding, and he and the boys turned a hefty profit knocking off houses and selling on the street. Life couldn't be sweeter, but life is a trip that often takes some unexpected turns. One evening, Pete and the boys had just broken into this big house in a high-class neighborhood. It wasn't five minutes after they broke in when they were confronted by the owner of the house, and if that wasn't terrifying enough, he was carrying a rifle. Two of Pete's buddies had hand-guns, but instead of pulling them, when the owner started shooting, they all ran. It was dark in the house, and they were bumping into stuff, but they kept running, and he kept shooting. They all made it out and kept on running. They wanted to get as far from that house as they could. When they finally did stop about three blocks away to catch their breath, one of the boys noticed the back of Pete's shirt was covered with blood. He had been hit, and he didn't even know it. Pete needed help, and he needed it fast. So they had to go back and get the car. They came in, all the while hoping that home owner wasn't still out there, looking for them. It took them nearly ten minutes, but they found the car, and not a moment too soon. By the time they found it, Pete was hurting really bad and getting weak and light-headed from the loss of blood.

By the time they got to the hospital, they had their story straight. They would tell the doctors that Pete's friend was cleaning his own rifle and it went off, striking Pete in the back. It was fool-proof unless the hospital cops began to search the hospitals, look-ing for a wounded burglary suspect. All of them were holding their breath the whole time.

The hospital patched Pete up and sent him home after four hours. They said his wound was just a little nick and looked a lot worse than it really was. Even so, Pete didn't think any of them exhaled until the car left the hospital parking lot and they were on the highway, headed home. Evidently, that guy didn't even realize he shot Pete because the police never came to the hospital looking for a gunshot victim. The bullet didn't kill Pete, and the cops didn't arrest him. Pete dodged two bullets that night.

Coming that close to death would have changed most people, but not him. Instead of waking him up and turning him around, it actually gave him a sense of invincibility, like nothing could harm him. Pete even became less fearful of death. He tried more things, took more chances. He told himself, *You only live once!* His think-ing was: "If you can live though getting shot, you can live through anything."

Pete kept going on with that way of thinking and living: drug dealing, burglary, petty theft. Things were going quite well. He always had money and could do pretty much anything he wanted. He enjoyed thinking of himself as being on a rocket to the moon, and it was true. Things were going up for him. The only problem with that is that everything that goes up eventually comes down, and sometimes, if you don't have the right directions, you could be head-ing toward one thing when you think you're heading toward another. Pete didn't know that then, but that was the very ride he was on.

One particular Thursday afternoon, he and some friends were headed to the Sub Shop to get some lunch. When they got there, they got word that Frank had gotten killed last night. Frank was one of the guys that had taken Pete to the hospital after they broke into that house. When he asked how it happened, they told him some-body robbed him. First, they shot Frank, then they stole his money and all the drugs he was carrying. After that, they just left him lying in the alley where he went down. Apparently, he laid there most of the night until somebody finally saw him and called the cops.

Losing somebody close like that had a strange effect on Pete. It kind of shook him up a little. It made him think. His confidence level went down a bit. It was just too close. He tried to put it behind him, and he did continue with his daily routine, but he couldn't seem to shake that nauseous feeling in his gut. That feeling that his whole world was closing in on him, caving in, if you will, and there was nothing he could do but wait it out.

Pete didn't have to wait too long. One day, on a Tuesday afternoon, Pete was carrying out his business as usual, selling drugs on the street. He was approached by this one guy, a new guy. Pete had never seen him before. He figured he was new to the neighborhood. When Pete gave him the dope, he reached for his money, pulled out a gun, and shouted, "You're under arrest!" Pete started to run, but when he did, two more cops were running toward him with their weapons drawn. Pete was busted cold.

For selling drugs and carrying an illegal weapon, the judge gave Pete fifteen years. Prison life was hard. As tough as he thought he was, it seemed like everybody else was a whole lot tougher. Making the adjustment from total freedom to daily confinement was extremely stressful too. Everything about prison life was difficult. The one bright side was the weekly church services. Pete first started going because it gave him two hours of free time. No restrictions. Nobody picking at him. Nobody messing with him. Nobody starting fights. It was kind of relaxing. He just sat there, sang some songs, and listened to this guy talk. At first, what he said didn't make a lot of sense to Pete. Then the preacher talked about God loving and caring for Pete. He figured, *I didn't need God's help.* He had always taken care of himself, but then he realized, *Taking care of myself is how I got in jail. It's how I got shot and could have died.* Maybe he wasn't doing such a good job. Then the preacher read a scripture from Isaiah 1:18, "Come now, and let us reason together, saith the Lord: though your sins be scarlet, they shall be as white as snow; though they be red like crimson, they shall be as wool."

When the preacher read that, it was as if God was speaking directly to Pete. God was telling him to look back over his life. Were there any bad things? Were there any wrong things? Was there any sin? Of course, there were, but God's message to Pete was, "This is a chance to make a change, to make things different." He was willing to accept Pete's past and give him a bright future.

Pete took the Lord up on His offer. If God was willing to accept a person like Pete, then maybe he was worth something. He accepted Christ as his Lord and Savior.

Pete thanks God He made a change in his life. He's not the same. He's a brand-new Pete. He's still in prison but no longer bound by prison walls.

Who Will Deliver Me?

For over twenty-five years, Josephine Perkins was the owner of a very successful corner store. Running a business seemed to come naturally to her. Every day, she looked forward to taking care of her regular customers and having all of the things they depended on. Of course, there were always new people in the neighborhood that she was always excited to meet and to serve their needs. She even found that the paperwork part of a business that many people find boring and unappealing was really not that bad. Auntie Jo's Corner Grocery had become a necessary staple in her community, and she was always proud to serve. For a quarter of a century, she delivered food products and other needs to the people of her community, but she would soon learn a very important lesson, one that would completely change her life and give her a new hope for the future. Even the best giver will need to be received at some point.

Mostly everybody in her close-knit community came to Auntie Jo's for their shopping needs, and it gave her an opportunity to meet folks, talk with them about their problems and daily events, and even see little babies grow up. She was on a first name basis with almost everyone that patronized her store, and she even knew a little of their family history. That's how it was in a small town like theirs. Auntie Jo's was open every day from 9 to 9 except Sunday. Josephine loved her work, she had good staff, and the business was quite successful. Because the business did so well, she was able to serve the community in other ways. A while back, she started a clothing drive to help the less fortunate in her community, as well as in the surrounding areas. It started out small at first—back then she only had about six or seven people working with her—but over the past twelve years, it has grown to over one hundred volunteers and five other businesses that support this cause. For the past five years, Josephine has been initiating a back-to-school campaign. This organization gathers school supplies and backpacks for children whose parents can't afford to get them. This too, has been well supported by the community.

Josephine truly loved what she did. Her business was going quite well. It gave her a chance to interact with people on a daily basis, and of course, the charities that she started had a very positive effect on those that needed her help. Now, far be it from her to say that she had the Midas touch—you know, where everything you touch turns to gold—but she will say that for her, life did have a certain upswing to it. Still, even when you hit a home run and everybody cheers, that ball will eventually come down at some point and hit the ground.

Having a small business as Josephine did, she handled all of the business end, but she also liked to be sort of a hands-on type of person. She was never above stocking shelves, organizing products, taking inventory, or even sweeping the sidewalk. Sitting in an office most of day was never her style.

But one particular day in April, she found herself getting winded doing a little cleaning, which was something she had always done. She imagined it was a little cold or something, which was also a little strange for her because she never got sick. *But,* she thought to herself, *everybody gets sick every once in a while.* So she took some cold medicine and went back to work, but it didn't seem to get better. Over time, she got even more tired. After a while, it was all she could do to get home and flop on the bed. This was not like her. She knew she was getting older, but she wasn't that old, and really, the more she thought about it, the less it seemed like old age. This seemed like it might be something else. She tried not to think about it too much because it made her nervous, but she came to the conclusion that the sooner she did something to fix this, the sooner it would get straightened out.

That Monday, she made an appointment with her primary care physician. Josephine told her all of the symptoms, how she was feeling tired, and how she got winded so easily. Josephine was hoping for some kind of pill, a quick fix, but the physician decided to run some tests on her. A lot of tests. A whole lot of tests. After that, Josephine was referred to a specialist. Oh, great. Another doctor! Josephine was hot. She didn't have time for all this, but even through her anger, one thing kept ringing in her ears. She was still feeling bad, and she didn't have any answers, so she decided to go along with the doctor's plan.

When Josephine got to this specialist, the first thing he did was order more tests. She thought, *Wonderful! Here were go again.* He gave her an appointment to come back three days later, when all the test results were in. Those might have been the worst three days of Josephine's life. Running a store, feeling extremely tired, and waiting for those test results at the same time made three days feel like three years!

When she finally got to the doctor's office, his findings hit her like a ton of bricks. He had seen a spot on Josephine's lung—a rather large one. She was going to need surgery. He said a lot of stuff after that, but she didn't hear it. All she kept hearing was "Spot on your lung," and "surgery!" What in the world was happening? She didn't have time for this. She had a business to run, charities she was in charge of. She couldn't afford to be out flat on her back for months.

As devastating as these feelings were, a worse thought came to her: *Suppose the operation doesn't go well. Suppose they can't fix my problem. Suppose this is the beginning of my end.* A weird feeling began to creep over her, like it was a dream, but it wasn't a dream. A surreal feeling. So many people counted on her, so many people depended on her, and she was always there for them. Now, the tables had turned. Now, she was in need. Now, she was suffering. She had fixed so many problems for others. These doctors had some answers, but their answers didn't address her fears, only her sickness, and she wasn't even sure that they could fix that. Somehow, for some reason, she felt like all these physicians weren't giving her what she really needed. She needed help. She needed support. She needed peace.

The day finally came when she was to have her surgery. She had to be at the hospital at seven in the morning. Surgery was scheduled for 9:00 a.m. She'd never felt so alone in her life. In a room filled with doctors and nurses preparing her for her operation, she felt like she was the only one in the place. Her face must have been showing what was in her heart because one of the nurses noticed her anguish when she came in to have Josephine sign some papers. She put the papers down and asked if she could pray with her. Josephine was a little surprised by her words, so she asked, "Why? I mean, what good is prayer now? I'm already scheduled for surgery."

She said, "Prayer might calm this. Give you a little peace."

Her words, more than anybody else's, seemed to be exactly what Josephine needed to hear. She said, "Go ahead and pray. I really do need some peace right now." The nurse prayed, and for the first time in weeks, Josephine did feel calm. A sense of peace really did come into the room.

After the nurse prayed, she said, "I have one more question. Do you know Jesus as Lord and Savior?"

Now, Josephine knew what this was. This was that church rhetoric that she had been hearing all of her life. Josephine never had time for church. She was always too busy, but you know, being flat on your back and facing risky surgery has a way of opening up your mind to new ideas. After all, the prayer did make her feel better. She had always been everybody's rock, everybody's deliverer, but now she needed a deliverer.

They prayed again, and Josephine accepted Jesus as her Lord and Savior. Suddenly, she had inner peace. Real peace. Not just that good feeling she got when she fed the homeless or gave out clothes. That was a good feeling, but that came when she did something for somebody. This new peace came straight from God, and she didn't have to work for it or do anything to earn it.

From that point on, Josephine had peace. It may have been the most relaxed she had ever been. She even had a sense of joy in her heart as they rolled her down the hall to surgery, and when she woke up in recovery, she gave God the praise for bringing her through. The doctors and nurses did a fine job. Josephine laughingly said to herself, *They were the best help money could buy, but what the Lord gave me, no amount of finances could purchase that.* He gave her peace, joy, and love, and the real healing came from His hands. This is a statement she always lives by, "The doctor can be my surgeon, but only God can be my deliverer."

The Race for Life

Jeremiah Jones, J. J. for short, was the biggest name in track-and-field the town had ever heard of. They had one of the best teams in the state, and Jeremiah was the star attraction. He competed in quite a few events on his high school team—the long jump, triple jump, and the high hurdles—but his best two events, the ones everybody was talking about, and the ones that kept his name in the papers, were the one hundred-meter and two hundred-meter dash. Running always came really easily to him. As a kid, he was the second fastest in his elementary school. In middle school, he was the fastest, and in high school, he was state champion in the one hundred and two hundred-meter dash in his junior and senior years. He had enough awards, trophies, and medals to cover most of the wall in his bedroom. With all that, along with the fact that his grades were pretty good, a B average, the scholarships just came pouring in. He had offers from some fairly big schools, a full four-year ride. He was truly living his dream, and that was a really good thing. The only downside to a dream is that at some point, you have to wake up.

Jeremiah took one of the schools about three states over. He liked it because it was a pretty nice-sized school that had a big focus on sports. He especially liked them because their track team did very well nationally. His thinking was, "To be the best, you've got to learn from the best."

Looking back, he now realizes that he couldn't have made a better decision. His coaches worked him from the time he got there, and his teammates weren't any joke either. When he was in high school, he was the standout, but it became clear to him that at the college level, everybody here was a high school standout. It was a kind of humbling experience, but Jeremiah had to put his pride aside and take his position as a track understudy.

Jeremiah took his time and kept his eyes and ears open to take in everything he could, and it wasn't long before he moved from his understudy position to a prominent member of the team. In high school, he had participated in several events, but now, his concentration was on the one hundred and two hundred-meter dash. Some might not realize it, but there's a lot of work involved in track-and-field. Working out in the weight room, learning new techniques for running, eating right, and having the right mental state are all part of doing your best on the track.

By his second year, Jeremiah began to win a few races. His coach said he was showing some excellent improvement, and that he should continue with his strenuous workout plan. He said to Jeremiah, "Who knows? If you keep up this pace, a national title, or even the Olympics could be in your future." The coach's words were very encouraging, but Jeremiah didn't want to get a swollen head. He figured that the best thing for him was to keep his head clear and just focus on the next race.

College wasn't all work, however. For a little change of pace, and just for fun, Jeremiah and a couple of friends joined the campus gospel choir. Jeremiah was never much one for church, but he did enjoy singing, and the other choir members were good folks. It was only for fun at first, singing and going to different places, but after a while, he actually looked forward to his time with the choir. Just being around these people made him feel good, sort of like a family. It wasn't long before he began to feel closer to the members of the choir than some people on the track team. Maybe it was because track was so much work, the choir was so much fun, and the songs they sang were so uplifting and joyful. Again, Jeremiah was never much into church, but those songs they sang did make him feel really good, and they got him thinking about his whole life and how he was living.

His next track meet was a tough one. They were going against a school that had an awesome track team, and they had been extremely good for several years. This team had produced twelve Olympians, and this year, their wins were the best in the conference. Yes, they were going to be tough to beat, but their coach told them all week, "Everybody needs to do their part, and if you do your part to the best of your ability, that's all you need to win."

You see, track is a little different from other sports. Track is a team sport made up from individual sports, so when the coach said, "Do your best," Jeremiah's part was the one hundred and two hundred-meter dash. That was his part, to win in his two events, and he came pretty close. He did win the two hundred-meter dash and was a very close second in the one hundred. He was satisfied with that. He had done what was asked of him. He gave it everything he had. He had given his best. Normally, when Jeremiah came away with a win, he was overjoyed, but this particular time, for some reason, it didn't mean as much. Something was lacking. He wasn't as happy as he usually was. It was weird. He'd never had this feeling before. He thought to himself, *Am I sad about something?* He thought about his friends. *No, I'm cool with them.* He thought about schoolwork. *No, my grades are okay. Well, maybe I need to get out and relax. No, that couldn't be it. I do hang out with the fellows, and I'm currently dating someone.* What was it? Was he losing his love of track? That couldn't be it, but something had definitely changed.

That week in practice, one of the girls on the relay team pulled a leg muscle and was going to be out for a while until her injury got better. Now, Jeremiah had seen injuries all the time—leg injuries, groin injuries, foot, back, arm and shoulder injuries—he'd even had a few himself. Most weren't serious, some were. Being an athlete, this was just part of the game. For whatever reason, though, her injury stayed in Jeremiah's mind. He was thinking thoughts like, *Suppose I get hurt and can't run anymore? I could lose my scholarship and have to leave the school. What then? All my plans would be crushed.* Jeremiah was counting on track to make it big. What would happen to him if track was suddenly over?

Feelings of delusion and fear haunted him all week. Fear that his career would end with one bad injury. Delusion because track didn't seem to offer the same happiness. It was so confusing and stressful.

It must have been showing on Jeremiah's face when he got to choir rehearsal because one of the girls asked him, "What in the world is wrong with you?" Jeremiah told her he was fine, but she didn't go for it. "J. J.," she said, "what's really wrong?" So he confessed that he had been a little down. Nothing seemed as much fun as it used to be. Nothing seemed to be exciting anymore. All of the stuff that used to make him happy just didn't now. It was like he lost something, but he didn't know what it was. She said to him, "I think I know what it is. Jesus is drawing you closer to Him, and the closer you get to Jesus, other things just aren't as special anymore." As much as Jeremiah wanted to disagree with her, what she said did make a lot of sense. He had been singing Christian songs. He had been going to church and hearing about God's love.

Jeremiah asked her, "What do I do now?"

She said, "Accept Jesus as Lord and Savior. He can give your joy back. All that you lost, you can find it in Him." So they prayed. In fact, the whole choir prayed with them. Jeremiah asked Jesus to be his Savior, and by the end of that prayer, his joy came back. His peace came back, but not like before. This time it was multiplied by a thousand. This time, he found himself in a new race. Now, he was running for Jesus.

Lori's Special Gift

For the past seven months, Lori had been planning and anticipating the most exciting time in a woman's life: her wedding. What made it even more special was that she was engaged to the most wonderful, the most charming, and the most sophisticated man of her dreams, Richard Evans.

Two years ago, she met him at an office party at her girlfriend's job. Soon after that, they started dating, and before long, their whirlwind romance took off. Richard had shown himself to be the most perfect man for her. He talked to her every day. If not in person, he called on the phone. He sent "I love you" text messages and emails all the time. He never forgot a birthday, or any holiday for that matter, and it's not just the big things that she loved about him. He's warm, sensitive, and he made sure she had everything she could possibly need, even before she asked for it. Richard was the most thoughtful man she had ever met. He was her breath of fresh air, and she's due for one after some of the bums and knuckleheads she had been dating in the past. That's why she felt so special because Richard was so different. Whatever it was, it's quite apparent to her that she was in a very good place in her life right now. A perfect place. The place for which she's waited for a long time.

Lori never knew that there was so much to do when planning a wedding—so many details, so many things to get straight, so many things to work out, and so many things that can go wrong. Between her 9-5 job and coming home and making wedding plans, it seemed like there weren't enough hours in a day. She never imagined so much work had to go into working out the details of an hour-long event. It would be a whole lot easier to go to the justice of peace and get it over with, but who wants easy? She had been planning this day her whole life. Richard was just the last piece of the puzzle—or the best piece. She was just overworked, excited, and stressed out all at the same time.

Again, Lori had been working on this for seven months, and the wedding wasn't until next year. They were planning for a pretty nice-sized wedding, about three hundred people. That's not too bad when you consider that they started out with five hundred guests. Richard and Lori knew a lot of people. That's why they put the wedding off for so long, so they would have enough time. It was beginning to seem like they didn't plan for enough time. That was okay. They'd figure it out somehow.

One day, about a couple of months ago, as Lori was up to her neck in job and wedding-related issues, she woke up one morning feeling totally nauseated. Not wanting to get behind in her office paperwork, she decided just take something for nausea and go to work. She told herself, *Lori, it's just a little upset stomach. You know you haven't been eating right. But lunchtime you'll be fine.*

And she was, but the next morning, it was the same thing! The same tiredness, the same nausea, the same dragging herself out of bed. That's when it came to her. Maybe this wasn't a virus. Maybe this wasn't some bad potato salad. Maybe she needed something other than another dose of Pepto-Bismol.

That evening after work, Lori stopped by the drugstore and bought a pregnancy test. Sure enough, that was it. She was pregnant! Lori was elated and scared at the same time. *How is Richard going to take the news?* she asked herself. *Will he be pleased or freaked out?* She was a little freaked out herself, but one call to her fiancée put her troubled mind to rest. He was overjoyed and couldn't wait to get together for a special celebration. *Isn't life grand?* Lori thought.

Of course, this meant that they had to push the wedding back a bit. All that they were dealing with, plus planning for the new baby, was a little too much. Still, nine months later, things couldn't have been better. They had a new baby boy, Richard Michael Evans Jr., six pounds, fifteen ounces, and the joy of his mommy and daddy's lives. It took a lot of doing, but they got everything ready for the new baby, and surprisingly, weren't too behind on the wedding plans. It was stressful, but it was a good stress, if there is such a thing.

About a month or so after Lori got her new baby home, she began to notice things about him. She couldn't quite put her finger on it. It was just that things didn't seem quite right. At first, she thought it must be post-pardon depression, you know, like a lot of women get. Over time, though, she knew that couldn't be it. It was the baby. Something was wrong with the baby. Lori spoke to Richard about it, and he felt they should let a doctor check the baby out. Richard said, "Whatever it is, if they catch it early enough, they can fix it." So they made an appointment with the pediatrician.

After a full examination of everything that doctors do, the doctor gave them the results. Lori's baby, her sweet precious little man, had Down syndrome. The doctor said a lot of stuff after that, but that was all she heard. This was impossible. This could not be happening. He was so perfect. He hadn't done anything wrong. It wasn't fair. Or maybe, maybe it was her. Something she did. Something she ate. Maybe she didn't do something right. The doctor assured Lori that it was nothing like that. It was just one of those things that happen. Lori heard what he said, but his words did little to put the air back in her lungs or calm the pounding in her head.

As they left his office, he gave them some information they would need and some people they could contact, but nothing to help with the pain in Lori's chest. Her heart ached for her son. When they got home, she and Richard both broke down. They were totally devastated.

Lori knew she had to pull herself together. She had to be strong for herself and her son. Things went on as usual for a while, but Lori was noticing that Richard wasn't coming around as much. She needed his help and his strength, but he started giving her all these excuses. He had to work late. He had to go out of town for his job. His car needed some work. It was always something. Then he started not answering her calls, and when she would leave a message, he wouldn't call back. What in the world was going on?

After a few days of this, Lori finally saw his car pull up in the driveway. "Good. It's about time. Just wait until he gets in this house." She had a few choice words for this guy. As soon as he came through the door, she let him have it. "Where have you been? What do you mean, not answering my calls? What's gotten into you? Have you lost your mind?!" The whole time she was ranting and raving, Richard never said a word. In fact, he looked absolutely expressionless.

When Lori asked him to explain himself, he simply said, "I'm done. I can't take this. I'm leaving town." And with that, he walked out of the front door, got in his car, and drove away. Lori was so stunned at what he had said that she couldn't even speak. She just stared at him as his car rolled down the street, turned the corner, and disappeared. Her heart was pounding, but she couldn't cry. *What just happened?* she asked herself. *Did he really just walk out on me? On us? We were about to be married. We have a son! Is this really it?*

Lori literally had a thousand questions, but no answers. She cried so much that her whole body began to feel weak. That night, she called her mother. She was at her wits' end. Her mother had always been a strong woman. Lori had seen her go through some tough times in her life, but she always got through them.

Her mother said, "With faith in God and prayer, I can do anything." Lori talked to her for the longest time, telling her that she didn't know what to do, she couldn't believe Richard left her, and she needed his help to her raise this child. She went on and on for at least three hours. Lori's mother listened, gave advice, and listened some more. By the end of the conversation, she told Lori, "You know, Lori, you really need to get back in the church. You kind of got away from the Lord. Why don't you go down and have a talk with the pastor? He's always counseling people in need, and maybe he can put you in touch with some help for little Ricky." It was true. Lori had gotten away from church, and for a time, she felt like she was doing fine without it, but now, she saw that her mom was right. She needed all the help she could get for herself and baby Ricky.

Lori made an appointment with the pastor on Tuesday evening. He was very welcoming, and he listened to all she had to say. She expressed to him how angry she was at this whole situation, and how bad it feels to drop so low after flying so high. "Pastor," Lori said, "I feel like God is angry with me, you know, for not coming to church. Maybe that's why my son is like he is."

He said to her, "Lori, God's not mad at you. He loves you. Think about it like this. God gave you a baby with Down syndrome, not because He's upset with you, but because He knew you were the kind of person that was strong and loving enough to give this baby a good life with a good mother. Little Ricky is not your punishment or burden. He is your special gift from God. He gave Ricky to you because He knew He could trust you with this child." Then he gave her a scripture from Proverbs 3:5–6: "Trust in the Lord with all thine heart, and lean not unto thine own understanding. In all thy ways acknowledge Him, and He shall direct thy paths."

They had a prayer, and Lori rededicated her life back to God. She left his office with a new sense of drive and purpose, but most of all, a relieving sense of forgiveness. God had accepted her back, and Lori did find help. The pastor had given her some phone numbers of some wonderful counseling and training programs that were a blessing to her and her son. Her whole situation is turning around for the good, one day at a time. Ricky really is Lori's special gift from God. She now thanks God for giving her son to her, but she especially thanks Him for giving her His Son.

About the Author

Shelton H. Smith Jr. is the pastor of Mount Moriah United Church of Christ in Waverly, Virginia. He was first called to ministry in April of 1990, when the Lord revealed that His will for Shelton's life is to preach and teach the Gospel. Since then, he has formed several ministries, including a prison ministry, nursing home ministry, and marriage seminar. His realistic approach to sharing God's message has touched lives and led many to Christ.

In 1987, Shelton married the love of his life, Marie. Together, they have two children, Ashley Christian and Shelton III. He and his wife reside in Chesapeake, Virginia, and they enjoy speaking for services and community programs.